POLICE
Search &
RESCUE!
SERVE & PROTECT

State Troopers

W9-CNA-247

by Meish Goldish

Consultant: Captain David R. Bursten
Chief Public Information Officer
Indiana State Police
Indianapolis, Indiana

BEARPORT
PUBLISHING

New York, New York

Credits

Cover and Title Page, © Holbox/Shutterstock, © Palino Spisiak/Shutterstock, and © Bikeriderlondon/Shutterstock; 4–5, © mikecphoto/Shutterstock; 4B, © Brandon Seidel/Shutterstock; 5R, Courtesy of the Iowa Department of Public Safety; 6–7, © Riccardo Piccinini/Shutterstock; 7, © Iowa Department of Public Safety; 8, © H. Mark Weidman Photography/Alamy Stock Photo; 9L, © Jimmy May/Associated Press; 9R, Courtesy of the Indiana State Police; 10, Courtesy of the Arkansas State Police; 11, © Jens Molin/Shutterstock; 12, © Mall Themd/Shutterstock; 13, © Jheric1983/Dreamstime; 14, © Monika Wisnlewska; 15L, © Ingram Publishing/Thinkstock; 15R, © itsjustme/Shutterstock; 16, © RICK WILKING/Reuters/Corbis; 17, © MATT MILLS MCKNIGHT/epa/Corbis; 18, © Elaine Thompson/AP/Corbis; 19, © Joshua Trujillo, Seattle P-I; 20L, © pavla/Shutterstock; 20–21, Courtesy of the New York State Police; 22, © Design Pics Inc/Alamy; 23L, Courtesy of the Indiana State Police; 23R, Courtesy of the Indiana State Police; 24, © Peter Steiner/Alamy; 25, Courtesy of the New York State Police; 26, © Ailin Li; 27, © John Wagner/ZUMA PRESS/Newscom; 28T, © Michael Matthews/Police Images/Alamy; 28BL, © Travis Heying/MCT/Newscom; 28BR, © Marc Duncan/Associated Press; 29T, © Zerbor/Shutterstock; 29M, © Volodymyr Krasyuk/Shutterstock; 29BL, © Vladimir L./Shutterstock; 29BR, © Brad Sauter/Shutterstock.

Publisher: Kenn Goin
Editor: Jessica Rudolph
Creative Director: Spencer Brinker
Photo Researcher: We Research Pictures, LLC.

Library of Congress Cataloging-in-Publication Data

Names: Goldish, Meish, author.
Title: State troopers / by Meish Goldish.
Description: New York, NY : Bearport Publishing, [2016] | Series: Police: search & rescue! | Includes bibliographical references and index.
Identifiers: LCCN 2015040035| ISBN 9781943553150 (library binding) | ISBN 1943553157 (library binding)
Subjects: LCSH: Police, State—Juvenile literature. | Rescue work—Juvenile literature.
Classification: LCC HV7965 .G65 2016 | DDC 363.2/332—dc23
LC record available at http://lccn.loc.gov/2015040035

For more information, write to Bearport Publishing Company, Inc., 45 West 21st Street, Suite 3B, New York, New York 10010. Printed in the United States of America.

10 9 8 7 6 5 4 3 2 1

Contents

A Sudden Stop

One day in May 2015, Iowa State Trooper Tracy Bohlen was on **patrol** on a busy highway when a pickup truck ahead of him suddenly stopped in the middle lane. The officer saw someone in the truck climb into the driver's seat. Then the vehicle took off briefly before stopping again. What was happening?

The truck stopped in the middle of a three-lane highway near Des Moines, Iowa.

Trooper Bohlen was driving on **Interstate** 35. This highway runs from Texas all the way to Minnesota.

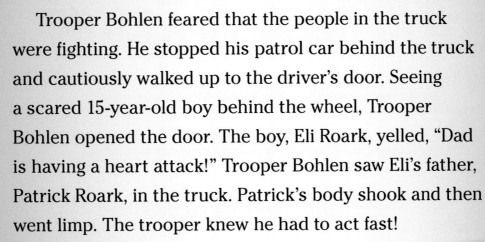

Trooper Bohlen feared that the people in the truck were fighting. He stopped his patrol car behind the truck and cautiously walked up to the driver's door. Seeing a scared 15-year-old boy behind the wheel, Trooper Bohlen opened the door. The boy, Eli Roark, yelled, "Dad is having a heart attack!" Trooper Bohlen saw Eli's father, Patrick Roark, in the truck. Patrick's body shook and then went limp. The trooper knew he had to act fast!

This picture, taken from a video camera inside Trooper Bohlen's police car, shows the officer approaching the truck.

A Dangerous Rescue

Trooper Bohlen felt Patrick's body for a **pulse** but couldn't detect one. With no time to waste, the officer called an ambulance and then pulled the **victim** out of the truck. The trooper immediately began to perform **CPR** on Patrick in the middle of the highway. At first, he feared the two of them might be hit by a passing car. However, when the officer looked up, he saw that all traffic had come to a stop.

After doing CPR for one minute, the trooper felt a pulse on the victim. Soon after, an ambulance arrived to take Patrick to a hospital. Thanks to Trooper Bohlen's quick actions, Patrick's life was saved.

Trooper Bohlen

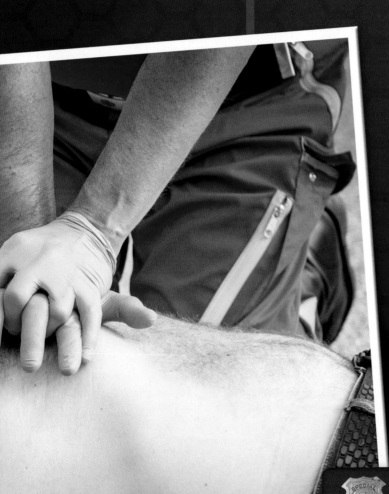

 Rescuers perform CPR when a person's heart stops beating or the victim has stopped breathing. They may press on the victim's chest and blow air into his or her mouth.

What Is a State Trooper?

Trooper Bohlen was doing an important job when he was patrolling Interstate 35. State troopers are police officers who work for the state. They work in areas that don't have local police departments, such as **rural** areas.

A state trooper driving in a rural area

State troopers have many **duties**, including important search-and-rescue work. The officers patrol state roads and highways, and respond to traffic accidents and other emergencies on roads. They try to prevent accidents by handing out tickets to people who are driving dangerously or too fast. In addition to keeping roads safe, the officers **investigate** crimes, such as robbery and the **illegal** sale of drugs and guns. Troopers also help victims of tornadoes, floods, and other **disasters**.

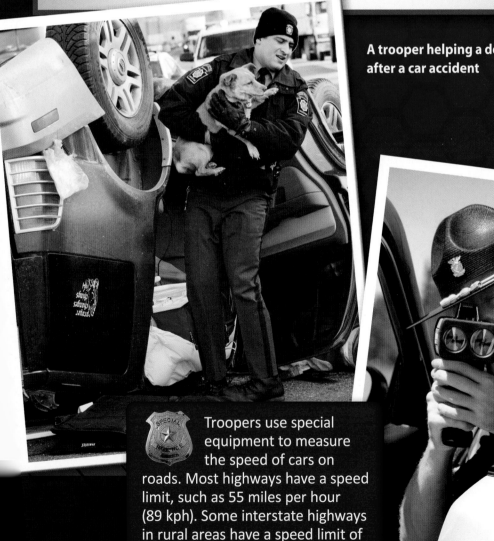

A trooper helping a dog after a car accident

Troopers use special equipment to measure the speed of cars on roads. Most highways have a speed limit, such as 55 miles per hour (89 kph). Some interstate highways in rural areas have a speed limit of 70 miles per hour (113 kph).

Training for the Job

To become a state trooper, a **recruit** must take a training course at a police academy. The program, which lasts up to six months, requires **trainees** to pass a number of tough physical tests. These include doing push-ups and sit-ups, plus running 1.5 miles (2.4 km), within a certain time period. Trainees must also be able to climb walls and lift heavy weights as practice for real-life rescues.

Trainees doing push-ups

To prepare for on-the-job rescues, recruits are taught how to give **first aid** to victims. Trainees learn how to bandage a wound to stop heavy bleeding. They also learn how to perform CPR on a person, in addition to other life-saving procedures. Every second counts during a rescue, so emergency medical training can save many lives.

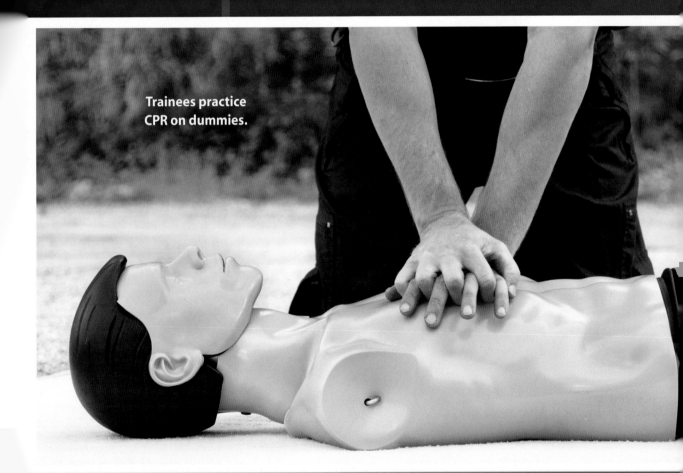

Trainees practice CPR on dummies.

At an academy, recruits also learn how to use weapons and how to

Trapped!

After their training is complete, state troopers are ready to help people in any emergency. One night in 2011, Oregon State Trooper Marc Boyd was driving past a home with a pickup truck parked in the driveway. In the dim light, it looked like a body was sticking out from under the vehicle.

Trooper Boyd spotted trouble one evening in a rural area.

Trooper Boyd stopped to check things out. When he got closer, he was alarmed by what he saw. He found Mike Martin, the truck's owner, with his head trapped under one of the tires! Mike had been checking a part under the vehicle when it rolled backward. The tire ended up on top of his head, pushing his face down into the gravel. Trooper Boyd saw that Mike was in terrible pain and barely able to talk. He needed help immediately.

The truck that Mike Martin was trapped under weighed about 6,000 pounds (2,722 kg)! Mike had been under the tire for about 20 minutes.

Mike was pinned under a truck similar to this one.

Very Thankful

Trooper Boyd called an ambulance and then ran to get a **tow strap** from his patrol car. He attached one end of the strap to the truck and the other end to his car. Then he slowly drove his car forward. The officer's plan worked! The heavy truck rolled off Mike's head.

Trooper Boyd used a tow strap to pull the truck off the victim.

Trooper Boyd was worried that Mike's skull was broken. Before the ambulance arrived, the officer kept speaking with the victim to make sure he didn't become **unconscious**. At the hospital, doctors performed surgery on Mike's ear and face. "My ear looks like a hamburger," he joked later, "but I'm okay." Mike was very thankful for the state trooper's quick rescue.

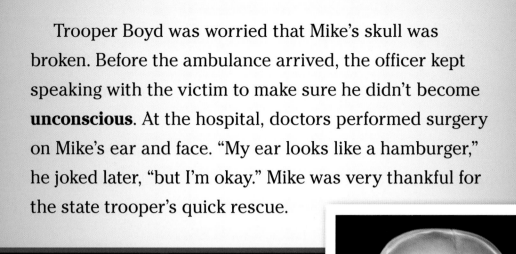

Amazingly, Mike's skull was not crushed under the weight of the car, and he suffered no injuries to his brain. Trooper Boyd said, "I cannot believe the human skull is that strong!"

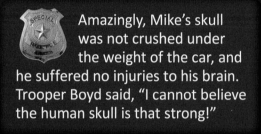

Mud Flood

Not all of a state trooper's rescues are made on roads. One morning in March 2014, part of a hill near Oso, Washington, **collapsed**, causing a giant **mudslide**. Within minutes, mud and **debris** flooded a rural neighborhood, knocking down trees and burying people and their homes.

Stillaguamish River

mudslide

Mud from the hill barreled over a neighborhood and into the Stillaguamish River.

Among the first rescuers to arrive at the disaster site was State Trooper Rocky Oliphant. He was shocked by what he saw. The mud, several feet high in some places, had pushed houses into a nearby street. Fallen trees and pieces of buildings were everywhere. Trooper Oliphant began searching for injured or trapped people. **Residents** told the trooper they could hear a voice in the distance calling for help—and they also heard a crying baby. A woman and her child were trapped in the mud!

The powerful mudslide destroyed 49 homes and other buildings.

A Path to Safety

Trooper Oliphant knew that a rescue attempt would be dangerous. He saw a power line sticking out of the mud near where the woman and baby were trapped. If the power line was **live**, it could **electrocute** anybody who came close to it. The trooper made sure the power was turned off, then he and other rescuers **waded** through the mud toward the victims. Trooper Oliphant tried to move as quickly as possible, but the thick mud—nearly up to his waist—slowed him down.

Rescuers at the scene of the mudslide

Finally, the rescuers reached the two trapped victims and pulled them out of the mud. Trooper Oliphant laid pieces of wood from destroyed houses on top of the mud to create an escape path for the rescuers and victims. After reaching solid ground, the mother and baby were taken to a hospital.

A Raging Fire

Sometimes, officers rescue people even when they're not on the job. In June 2014, a senior investigator with the New York State Police, John Vescio, was filling his car's tank at a gas station while he was off duty. Suddenly, another car sped into the station and crashed into a gas pump near the officer. The pump exploded into flames!

The car crash occurred after the driver, a 69-year-old man with **diabetes**, passed out behind the wheel.

Even though flames were shooting 15 feet (4.6 m) into the air, Investigator Vescio took action to help those in danger. He pulled the unconscious driver from his car seconds before it caught on fire. Then the officer remembered that his own car trunk held **ammunition** that might explode in the fiery heat. Quickly, he led other customers at the station away from the area. The off-duty officer bravely risked his own life to save the car-crash victim and many others.

Investigator Vescio's car

Deer in Trouble

State troopers don't just save the lives of people. Sometimes they rescue animals, too. One morning in May 2015, the state troopers office in Putnam County, Indiana, received several calls from drivers about a baby deer on a highway. The tiny fawn was in danger of being hit by a car. Trooper Mike Wood reported to the scene.

When deer cross the road, there is a danger to both the animals and drivers.

The officer saw the baby deer in the middle of the highway. Nearby was a dead adult deer, probably the baby's mother. Trooper Wood stopped his patrol car, picked up the little fawn, and wrapped it in a towel. Later, the baby was taken to an animal **rehabilitation center**. Thanks to Trooper Wood, the fawn was safe!

Trooper Wood placed the baby deer on the seat of his patrol car before driving to get help.

 Trooper Wood was happy that so many drivers cared enough to report what they saw on the highway. He said, "It was heartwarming for all of us to play such an important role in the health and well-being of this animal."

Trooper Wood with the fawn

23

On Thin Ice

In addition to helping wild animals, state troopers may risk their lives to rescue people's pets. In December 2014, Warren Smith was walking his dog, Belle, alongside a **canal** near Rochester, New York, when she got loose. The dog ran onto the canal's frozen surface and fell through the ice. State Trooper Kevin Lund heard a report about the dog on his police radio and drove to the canal.

Belle fell into icy water near this section of the Erie Canal.

Trooper Lund saw Belle struggling to keep her head above water, so he acted quickly. The officer crawled onto the ice and moved toward the dog. The ice cracked and popped under his weight. Then, the ice broke—and Trooper Lund fell into the freezing canal! Luckily, the brave trooper still managed to grab Belle, climb out of the water, and crawl across the ice to shore. Neither Belle nor Trooper Lund was injured.

Officers who make rescues in icy waters often wear special protective suits so they don't freeze. Trooper Lund did not have a suit, and was lucky to have survived. The freezing water could have caused him to

Trooper Lund (left) with Warren Smith, his wife, and their dog, Belle

Why Be a State Trooper?

Being a state trooper can be dangerous, so why would anyone want to become one? Missouri State Trooper Brandon Harris joined the force because he wanted to help people. The trooper makes sure all **citizens** are kept safe and treated fairly. "I try to talk to everyone with respect," he says. "Everybody is treated equally."

State Trooper Brandon Harris

Sergeant Amy Landy of New York State became an officer because of the job's excitement. While patrolling streets and highways, the sergeant has had her share of surprises. "I once delivered a baby girl on the side of the interstate!" With dedicated officers like Sergeant Landy and Trooper Harris, people know they can always count on the state police in times of need.

Many troopers enjoy taking time to read to kids. Some officers also teach school children about safety or about what it's like to be a state trooper.

State police departments are organized by **rank**. The rankings go up from a trooper—a basic officer—to corporal, sergeant, lieutenant, captain, major, and colonel. The person in charge of a state police department is called the Superintendent or Director.

State Troopers' Equipment

State troopers use special equipment when working. Here is some of their gear.

A *light bar* has flashing lights that can easily be seen so other drivers know to make room for the vehicle.

An *emblem* and a *label* identify the car as belonging to a state trooper.

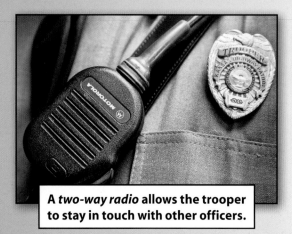

A *two-way radio* allows the trooper to stay in touch with other officers.

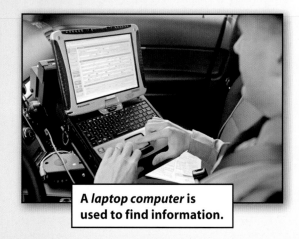

A *laptop computer* is used to find information.

A *first-aid kit* has bandages and other medical items that may be used to treat an injured person.

A *flashlight* is used for searches at night.

A *tow strap* is used to move a car after an accident.

Radar devices and other special equipment allow a trooper to identify which cars are going too fast.

Glossary

ammunition (*am*-yuh-NISH-uhn) objects, such as bullets, that are fired from weapons

canal (kuh-NAL) a human-made waterway

citizens (SIT-ih-zuhnz) people who live in a particular country, city, or town

collapsed (kuh-LAPSD) fell down or caved in

CPR (SEE-PEA-AHR) letters that stand for *cardiopulmonary resuscitation*; a type of rescue where a person blows air into the mouth and then presses down on the chest of someone whose heart has stopped

debris (duh-BREE) the scattered pieces of buildings or other objects that have been destroyed or damaged

diabetes (*dye*-uh-BEE-teez) a disease in which a person has too much sugar in his or her blood; it can cause a person to pass out

disasters (dih-ZASS-turz) events, such as floods, that cause terrible destruction

duties (DOO-teez) things required by one's job

electrocute (i-LEK-truh-kyoot) to kill with electricity

first aid (FURST AYD) care given to an injured or sick person before he or she is treated by a doctor

hypothermia (*hye*-puh-THUR-mee-uh) a condition in which a person's or an animal's body temperature drops dangerously low

illegal (i-LEE-guhl) against the law

interstate (IN-tur-stayt) a highway that runs between two or more states

investigate (in-VESS-tuh-*gayt*) search for information to find out about something

live (LYVE) carrying electricity

mudslide (MUHD-slyed) a large amount of mud or dirt that moves rapidly down a hill

patrol (puh-TROHL) the action of driving around an area to keep the area safe

pulse (PUHLSS) a steady beat or throb felt on a body indicating that the heart is pumping blood

rank (RANGK) an official position in a police force

recruit (ri-KROOT) someone who has recently joined a group

rehabilitation center (*ree*-huh-bil-uh-TAY-shuhn SEN-tur) a place where an animal is restored to good health

residents (REZ-uh-duhnts) people who live in a particular place

rural (RUR-uhl) having to do with the countryside; away from cities

shock (SHOK) a sudden disturbance of the body's functions

tow strap (TOH STRAP) a strip of leather or other material used to pull a car

trainees (tray-NEEZ) people who are being taught particular work skills

unconscious (uhn-KON-shuhss) passed out; unable to think, hear, feel, or see, often as the result of a serious illness or accident

victim (VIK-tuhm) a person who is hurt or killed

waded (WAYD-id) walked through shallow water or mud

Bibliography

Mauldin, William. *State Troopers of America: The Compendium of State Troopers.* Greensboro, NC: William Mauldin Productions, Inc. (2006).

Olsen, Marilyn. *State Trooper: America's State Troopers and Highway Patrolmen.* Paducah, KY: Turner (2001).

Read More

Aronin, Miriam. *Highway Patrol Officers (Police: Search & Rescue!).* New York: Bearport (2016).

Christopher, Nick. *What Do Police Officers Do? (Helping the Community).* New York: PowerKids Press (2016).

Ollhoff, Jim. *Police (Emergency Workers).* Edina, MN: ABDO (2013).

White, Nancy. *Police Officers to the Rescue (The Work of Heroes: First Responders in Action).* New York: Bearport (2012).

Learn More Online

To learn more about state troopers, visit
www.bearportpublishing.com/PoliceSearchAndRescue

Index

About the Author

Meish Goldish has written more than 200 books for children. His book *Animal Control Officers to the Rescue* was a Children's Choices Selection in 2014. He lives in Brooklyn, New York.